LITTLE ROCK

THE DESEGREGATION OF CENTRAL HIGH

BY LAURIE A. O'NEILL

Spotlight on American History
The Millbrook Press • Brookfield, Connecticut

To my parents, to the Little Rock Nine, and to
all who have been courageous in times of adversity.

Library of Congress Cataloging-in-Publication Data
O'Neil, Laurie, 1949–
Little Rock : the desegregation of Central High / by Laurie A. O'Neil.
p. cm. — (Spotlight on American history)
Includes bibliographical references (p.) and index.
Summary: In September 1957, a high school in Little Rock, Arkansas,
became a civil rights battleground when nine black students sought to
enroll. This book tells their story and explains its importance
in the broad context of the civil rights movement.
ISBN 1-56294-354-5
1. Central High School (Little Rock, Ark.)—History—20th century—
Juvenile literature. 2. School integration—Arkansas—Little Rock—
History—20th century—Juvenile literature. 3. Afro-American
students—Education, Secondary—Arkansas—Little Rock—History—20th
century—Juvenile literature. 4. Afro-Americans—Civil rights—
Arkansas. I. Title. II. Series.
LD7501.L6862054 1994 373.767'73—dc20 93-29057 CIP AC

Cover photograph courtesy of Arkansas History Commission.
Photographs courtesy of Arkansas History Commission: pp. 6, 35,
53; UPI/Bettmann: pp. 11, 22, 27, 30, 44 (left), 48, 55; Carl
Iwasaki, Life Magagzine © 1953 Time Inc.: p. 13; AP/Wide World
Photos: pp. 15, 24, 29, 39, 40, 44 (right); The Schomburg Center
for Research in Black Culture, New York Public Library: p. 18.

Published by The Millbrook Press
2 Old New Milford Road, Brookfield, Connecticut 06804

Contents

Little Rock

September 25, 1957: Federal troops stand guard as nine African-American students enter all-white Central High School in Little Rock, Arkansas.

1

ROADBLOCK ALPHA

It was a morning like no other in the history of Little Rock, Arkansas. A five-story brick and stone building in the heart of the city had become a battleground.

Lines of armed paratroopers stretched for two city blocks. Patrol jeeps drove up and down. Soldiers, their walkie-talkies crackling, watched from the rooftop. A military helicopter hovered overhead. Near the building, a normally quiet, tree-shaded intersection had been given the name Roadblock Alpha. Barriers had been set up, and troopers questioned anyone who tried to pass.

The building was Central High School. It was September 25, 1957, and U.S. troops had been sent to Little Rock to make sure nine black teenagers safely entered the formerly all-white school.

The mood was angry and tense as a riotous mob of white protesters pushed against the barricades. "Don't let the niggers in!" they shouted, using cruel and insulting words to describe the black students. Major James Meyers stood on a sound truck and ordered the crowd to disperse. "Clear this area immediately!" he demanded, but the protesters surged ahead. Suddenly Meyers called out an order and a line of troopers stepped forward, bayonets drawn. The crowd scattered.

Meanwhile a convoy was approaching the high school. Four Army jeeps filled with soldiers and outfitted with mounted machine guns escorted an olive-drab station wagon. Inside were nine nervous but excited black teenagers.

At 9:22 A.M. the station wagon pulled quickly to a stop in front of the school. Dozens of troopers immediately formed a tight guard around it. News cameras set up on the tops of cars and trucks began filming the scene. A chant arose from the crowd: "Two, four, six, eight! We don't want to integrate!" Faculty and staff members watched anxiously from the school windows.

The nine black students got out of the car and started up the series of steps that led to the school entrance. They walked in double file, a line of troopers on each side. Some twenty-five soldiers were already stationed inside the school. "Good morning," Principal Jess Matthews said to the nine. "You may go to your classes now."

The new students went off in different directions, each with an armed bodyguard. Outside, scores of reporters scrambled to file their stories. The school year at an integrated Central High School had finally begun.

What followed, however, were months of harassment and abuse for the teenagers, who came to be known as the Little Rock Nine. By focusing the attention of the country—and the world— on the issue of school desegregation, they would become symbols of the civil rights struggle.

2

SEPARATE BUT NOT EQUAL

The word desegregation conjures up many unpleasant scenes in American history of the 1950s and 1960s. At white schools and colleges across the southern United States, angry protesters tried, often successfully, to keep black students out, even when the law would allow them to enter.

Mostly this was due to a long-standing belief held by many people that whites were superior to blacks and that the races should be separated, or segregated. This attitude, called racism, had its roots in seventeenth century America, when the enslavement of black people began.

By the early 1800s slavery was flourishing in the South, where cotton, sugar, and tobacco plantations needed large numbers of workers. Slaves were treated as possessions that were bought and sold. They were denied basic rights such as property ownership and education.

After the Civil War, when slavery was abolished, freed blacks still suffered widespread discrimination. Their lack of education prevented them from getting good jobs. Despite new laws meant to prohibit racial separation, white people tried to hold onto segregation as a traditional part of their culture.

Many southern states adopted their own laws to enforce segregation. They were called Jim Crow laws, after a black character in a popular song-and-dance routine of the 1800s. The laws required separate facilities for black people. There were separate rest rooms and railway cars, separate hotels and hospitals, separate theaters and jails, separate elevators and drinking fountains, even separate entrances and exits from buildings.

In 1896, a landmark U.S. Supreme Court decision only made matters worse. It upheld the state laws that denied black people equal rights. When a black man, Homer Plessy, boarded a train in Louisiana and sat in a coach reserved for whites, he was arrested. Judge John H. Ferguson of the Criminal Court of New Orleans agreed with the Louisiana law, which provided black people with "separate but equal" accommodations on railway cars.

The Supreme Court upheld Judge Ferguson's opinion, saying that segregation was legal according to the Fourteenth Amendment to the Constitution, which guarantees all citizens equal protection under the law. The Court's ruling was then used to justify all types of segregated public facilities, including schools, for decades to come.

"Separate but equal," however, was rarely the case. Most black schools lacked the advantages of schools for whites. Per pupil spending by local and state governments for public school materials and teacher salaries was sometimes four times more for white students than for black.

During World War II, hundreds of thousands of blacks served their country in the U.S. military. These soldiers returned home

Before integration, schools provided for black children were rarely as good as those provided for whites. This one room shack in Farmville, Virginia, served as a makeshift school for black children after local officials closed public schools to avoid integration. White students, meanwhile, attended private schools that received state and county funds.

to find the same restrictions in jobs, housing, and schools as before. They were frustrated and angry. Public opinion about segregation began to change. Pressured by civil rights groups, the courts began slowly to make decisions that ended segregation in public places, including schools.

By far the most important federal court case was decided in 1954. Known as *Brown* v. *Board of Education of Topeka*, the ruling reached far beyond that Kansas city. The Supreme Court ordered that segregation in America's public schools must be ended.

The Reverend Oliver Brown of Topeka wanted to enroll his seven-year-old daughter, Linda, in an elementary school four blocks from his house. The child had been walking two miles, then waiting a half hour, sometimes in rain or snow, for a bus to her all-black school. But she was denied admission to the school that was nearer to her home because it was for white students only.

Brown sued the Topeka Board of Education, saying he was being denied equal protection under the law. His lawsuit was grouped with five similar suits by black parents against school districts in other areas. When arranged in alphabetical order, the name Brown came first and that is what the case was called.

The black parents were represented by attorneys from the National Association for the Advancement of Colored People, or NAACP, a civil rights organization. The case was argued before the Supreme Court by a highly respected black lawyer, Thurgood Marshall.

During the arguments, lawyers for the school districts told the Court that it should not interfere with what an individual state did. But Marshall spoke out strongly against segregation. "Ever since the Emancipation Proclamation, the Negro has been trying to get the same status as anybody else, regardless of race," he declared.

Linda Brown, whose father's suit against the Topeka Board of Education set the stage for integration of public schools.

THURGOOD MARSHALL

THURGOOD MARSHALL is considered America's most famous civil rights lawyer. The great-grandson of a slave, he was the first African American to serve on the United States Supreme Court.

Marshall was born in 1908 in Baltimore, Maryland. His mother, Norma, was a schoolteacher, and his father, William, a Pullman porter and a steward at a country club. Marshall went to local segregated schools and graduated with honors in 1930 from Lincoln University, an all-black college in Chester, Pennsylvania. He worked as a waiter and grocery clerk to pay his tuition.

Marshall attended law school at Howard University in Washington, D.C. He received his law degree in 1933, graduating at the top of his class.

For several years he worked for the NAACP, first as an attorney, then as head of its legal staff. Marshall traveled across the South representing thousands of clients in civil rights cases, some of whom were too poor to pay him.

He personally experienced the humiliation of racial discrimination, often sleeping and eating in his car when he was not allowed in hotels and restaurants. Marshall frequently faced hostility and danger; once he was nearly lynched.

As an attorney he won twenty-nine of thirty-two cases he argued before the Supreme Court, including one that integrated the University of Maryland Law School, which had refused him admission many years earlier because he was black. His reputation earned him the nickname "Mr. Civil Rights."

In 1954, Marshall successfully argued the most celebrated case of his career: *Brown* v. *Board of Education of Topeka.*

He helped convince the nine Supreme Court justices that racial segregation in America's public schools should be ended.

President Lyndon B. Johnson named Marshall the solicitor general of the United States in 1965. Two years later the president nominated Marshall to the Supreme Court, saying the nomination was "the right thing to do, the right time to do it, the right man and the right place."

A believer in change through nonviolence, Marshall was responsible for much of the progress of the civil rights movement in this century. He helped remove barriers to black people in schools, housing projects, courtrooms, and voting booths. A liberal Democrat, he was known for his honesty and straightforward way of speaking.

After retiring from the Supreme Court in 1991, Marshall died two years later at the age of eighty-four. He is buried in Arlington National Cemetery.

As chief counsel for the NAACP, Thurgood Marshall played an important role in the struggle to integrate Little Rock schools.

The nine justices knew their opinion would have a major impact on school desegregation all across the nation. When their decision was finally announced on May 17, 1954, it was unanimous. In a loud, clear voice, Chief Justice Earl Warren read the Court's ruling.

"To separate Negro children solely because of their race generates a feeling of inferiority . . . that may affect their hearts and minds in a way unlikely ever to be undone," he said. "The doctrine of 'separate but equal' has no place. Separate educational facilities are inherently unequal."

The stage was now set for integration of the country's public schools. But integration would not be accomplished quickly, or without resistance, disorder, and violence.

WITH ALL DELIBERATE SPEED

The Supreme Court decision enraged southern segregationists. Some called for Chief Justice Warren's impeachment. Several states vowed to abolish public schools in order to avoid desegregation. They passed new laws to help them sidestep the court order.

Many school districts simply ignored the decision or delayed any discussion of a desegregation plan. After all, they reasoned, the Court did not say when desegregation must start or how it should be accomplished.

Enforcement of the ruling was left to state and local officials. U.S. district courts were given the responsibility to see that desegregation was carried out.

By 1954, public school integration was already the law in most northern states. The vast majority of segregated schools were in the Deep South and in the southern border states of Delaware, Kentucky, Maryland, Missouri, Oklahoma, and West Virginia.

After the ruling, school districts in the border states and in Washington, D.C., began to integrate their schools. There were

In some areas, the idea of school desegregation prompted a violent reaction. This sign was put up by anonymous extremists in Florida in the late 1950s.

protests in the form of boycotts, threats, and harassment of black students, but officials in these states took quick action to punish anyone interfering with desegregation.

Except for two school districts in Arkansas and one in Texas, no other public schools in the South had yet been desegregated. In some southern communities that tried to comply with the ruling, active groups of segregationists protested and many whites withdrew their children from public schools. The opposition was strongest in states with the largest percentage of blacks and the most restrictive state and local segregation laws.

In Arkansas, however, few expected any trouble. It was not considered a Deep South state. After all, the University of Arkansas' law school had started admitting blacks several years earlier, as had its medical school and graduate center in Little Rock.

[18]

Little Rock, the capital and largest city of Arkansas, is situated on the Arkansas River in almost the geographic center of the state. In the mid-1950s, it had 120,000 residents, nearly a quarter of them black. Called the City of Roses, Little Rock was proud of its low crime rate and cleanliness.

Little Rock was considered progressive, even liberal, for a southern city. Though segregation was practiced in schools, restaurants, and waiting rooms, race relations were cordial. Racial incidents, which had plagued the city a decade before, were rare.

The city had several integrated neighborhoods. Blacks served on juries and in the police force, rode buses and trains with whites and shared the municipal library. A third of the city's eligible black residents had registered to vote, a high percentage for a southern state at the time.

Who could predict that Little Rock would be the scene of mob violence, of bombings and cross burnings? The community would soon be divided by hate and fear, and become a symbol of racial intolerance.

Five days after the *Brown* decision, the city's school board announced it would comply with the federal desegregation order, though its members were unhappy with the lack of direction provided by the Court. The superintendent of schools, Virgil Blossom, was asked to develop a desegregation strategy.

That summer Blossom drew up a preliminary plan for gradual desegregation. It would begin with two of the city's high schools that were then under construction and scheduled to open in 1956. Later, Little Rock's junior high and elementary schools would be integrated.

Work on the plan continued for months. Then, nearly a year after the *Brown* decision, the Court ruled again, this time that desegregation must be carried out "with all deliberate speed." Still, no deadline was set.

Soon after the second ruling, the school board adopted a different version of Blossom's plan. Desegregation would begin in 1957 with one high school and a limited number of students in grades ten, eleven, and twelve.

The city's black parents were upset. They saw this as a delaying tactic. Blossom explained that the board did not want to rush desegregation because such a sudden change would be traumatic for the city.

Angry families went to the local chapter of the NAACP for help. In February 1956, a lawsuit was filed on behalf of thirty-three black children and their parents, asking the federal district court to force immediate integration of all grades.

The court ruled in favor of the school board, saying that the Little Rock Phase Plan, as it was called, was "in good faith." The NAACP appealed, but in April 1957 the plan was again upheld. The school board was told, however, that it could delay integration no longer.

Blossom spent the next few months giving dozens of talks about the desegregation of Central High School. Opposition to the plan grew. People who opposed integration came from all over Arkansas and from other southern states to speak out against it. They showed up at school board meetings and made highly emotional statements that warned of the dangers of "race mixing."

Advertisements paid for by segregationists were run in local newspapers. "Will black and white students share the same rest rooms?" the advertisements asked. "Will they attend the same dances?" This kind of publicity inflamed the community, forcing residents to take sides on the issue and greatly damaging the cause of desegregation.

4

THE LITTLE ROCK NINE

At the end of the 1957 school year, teachers at all-black Horace Mann High and Dunbar Junior High collected the names of students interested in attending Central High. Through rigorous screening the board reduced the list to about seventy-five students who had superior academic records and no disciplinary problems.

In a move that some felt was meant to discourage the students, school officials warned the families of the black candidates that the teenagers might face serious problems adjusting to a formerly white school. Many parents, concerned for their children, talked them out of transferring.

School was to open on September 3. Several more candidates withdrew until only nine remained. Ernest Green, a National Honor Society member and Boy Scout Eagle Badge holder at Horace Mann, would be the only senior in the group.

Melba Patillo, Minniejean Brown, Elizabeth Eckford, Thelma Mothershed, Gloria Ray, and Terrance Roberts would be juniors at Central. Jefferson Thomas and Carlotta Walls would enter as sophomores.

The Little Rock Nine posed for this photo at the height of the
crisis. Seated on the floor are, from left, Thelma Mothershed,
Elizabeth Eckford, and Melba Patillo. Behind them are
Jefferson Thomas, Ernest Green, Minniejean Brown,
Carlotta Walls, Terrance Roberts, and Gloria Ray.

Shortly before school began, the candidates, accompanied by
their parents and Daisy Bates, president of the Arkansas NAACP,
attended a meeting with the superintendent of schools. There they
learned that at Central they would not be able to participate in
team sports, run for student office, join social or service clubs, play

with the two school bands, or attend dances. This was supposedly because they were transfer students but most likely, the nine realized, it was because they were black.

The nine had been active in extracurricular activities at their former schools. Ernest played tenor saxophone with a musical group called the Jazzmen, Jefferson excelled at track, and Carlotta was active in the junior National Honor Society and was vice president of the student council. They were very disappointed.

Still, they remained committed to their decision. Besides wanting to be a part of an important integration effort, they knew that Central had an excellent academic reputation and fine facilities, including well-equipped science labs. Though Horace Mann was a newer school, Central could offer them more resources and opportunities, from a variety of educational materials to a wide range of course options.

In the days before school began, Daisy Bates tried to prepare the nine for the adversity they faced. "Ignore racial slurs and avoid confrontations," she said. She tried to instill confidence in the small group of black teenagers who were about to make history. "Be strong and keep your dignity," she told them. "I know you can do it."

Trouble had been brewing in Little Rock all summer. In early August, several parents who opposed desegregation formed the Mothers League of Central High School. Another local segregationist group, the Capital Citizens Council (CCC), began urging Governor Orval Faubus to defy the federal integration order.

Eleven days before the opening of school, Governor Marvin Griffin of Georgia spoke at a dinner hosted in Little Rock by the CCC. He urged Arkansans to join Georgians in resisting integration. The audience of three hundred people cheered.

That night a rock was thrown through Daisy Bates's window, sending a shower of broken glass over the living room floor. A piece of paper was wrapped around the rock. "Stone this time," it read. "Dynamite next."

Daisy was no stranger to violence. Her mother had been murdered by white men when Daisy was a baby. She took a deep breath and looked at her husband, L. C. Bates. "We are at war in Little Rock," she said.

On Tuesday, August 27, the Mothers League filed a lawsuit in Arkansas Chancery Court to get a legal order, or injunction, against the integration of Central High. Governor Faubus appeared as a surprise witness at the public hearing. He had been told, he said, that black and white teenagers were buying guns and knives and planning to fight. The injunction was granted.

That night the segregationists in Little Rock celebrated, driving by Daisy's house and honking their horns. "Did you hear the news?" they yelled. "The niggers won't be going to Central!"

The NAACP immediately petitioned the court to cancel the injunction. There was no evidence of increased weapon sales nor had any threats of violence been made, they told the judge. He ordered that integration must proceed and that no one could interfere with it.

The *Arkansas Gazette*, a local paper, called for tolerance. "On Tuesday the world will see that we are a law abiding people," said an editorial. But this was not to be.

In the next few days an 8-foot (2.4-meter) fiery cross was burned on the Bateses' lawn. "Go back to Africa," said an attached message, "signed, the KKK," a reference to the Ku Klux Klan, a racist organization whose members often use violent means to intimidate blacks.

Over the weekend, NAACP representatives met with Superintendent Blossom, Little Rock Police Chief Marvin Potts, and Mayor Woodrow Wilson Mann. They discussed how the Little Rock Nine could be protected in case of trouble on Tuesday. Some fifty police officers, it was decided, would patrol the school and prevent crowds from forming. Everyone felt confident that this would take care of any problems.

From his office in the State House, however, the governor was about to level his own attack on integration. It would shock all of Little Rock and turn the first few days of school into a nightmare.

DON'T LET THEM SEE YOU CRY

Orval Faubus, forty-seven years old, was in his second term as governor of Arkansas. His popularity was slipping, and he needed new support in order to win a third term, something no other candidate for governor in Arkansas had been able to do for the past fifty years.

After the *Brown* decision, Faubus had not taken a stand on the desegregation issue. No one expected him to oppose the integration of Central High School.

During the summer, members of his administration began to pressure Faubus. "Do you want to be known as the governor who encouraged the mixing of the races?" they asked him. "You have the power to prevent integration," they said. "If you use it you'll become a great man."

Faubus made a decision. Desegregation would become his primary campaign issue. Arkansas was not ready, he would say. Forcing integration would ruin the "good" relationship enjoyed by whites and blacks and would only lead to trouble.

Hitting the campaign trail, Arkansas Governor Orval Faubus leads a parade designed to drum up support for a third term. The school desegregation issue became the centerpiece of his 1957 bid for reelection.

Monday, September 2, was Labor Day. That evening a reporter knocked on Daisy's door. "Do you know there are National Guardsmen all around Central High School?" he asked. Horrified, Daisy and L. C. jumped into their car and drove to the school. They saw hundreds of soldiers in full battle dress spilling out of army trucks.

On television that evening, Faubus made an announcement that stunned the city. Caravans of white supremacists were headed to Little Rock from all over, he said. If integration is carried out, he added, "blood will run in the streets."

"I have called out the National Guard," the governor said. "The soldiers will not act as segregationists or integrationists," he explained, "but will maintain order and protect the lives and property of citizens."

School officials held an emergency session that night. They decided the Little Rock Nine should stay home from school until the situation could be resolved.

The next morning a small crowd gathered at Central, which was surrounded by 250 soldiers. Inside there was disorder. Many white students had stayed home. The Guard had refused to admit the school's black kitchen and maintenance employees. Teachers and administrators were confused and upset.

Parents of the nine black students were frightened and worried about their children's safety. One mother, Birdie Eckford, a teacher at a state school for the blind, was particularly troubled. As a child she had witnessed a mob lynch and burn a black man in Little Rock.

Approached by the NAACP, the U.S. district court judge ordered integration to proceed. Superintendent Blossom met with the families of the Little Rock Nine. The black students would attend Central the next day, but their parents should not accompany them, he said, because their presence at the school might only incite violence.

Daisy called Chief Potts and asked for a police escort for the students. Then she began telephoning the nine teenagers to tell them to meet her a few blocks from the school. Two police cars would drive them the rest of the way. Daisy reached everyone but the Eckfords, who had no phone. She made a mental note to go to their home early the next day.

Central High Principal J. W. Matthews confers with officers of the National Guard, called in by the governor to block integration of the school.

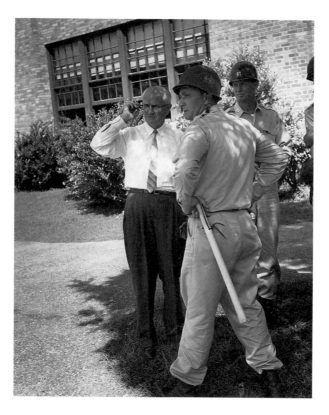

Elizabeth Eckford endures the taunts of an angry crowd outside Central High on September 4, 1957.

On Wednesday morning, Elizabeth Eckford put on the new white dress with black and white checkered trim that she had sewn for her first day at Central. The Eckfords prayed together. Then Elizabeth put on a pair of sunglasses, picked up her new green notebook and left the house. She headed for the public bus stop, unaware that the other eight students had gone to meet Daisy.

A mob had descended upon Central High, and hundreds of helmeted, grim-faced soldiers stood shoulder to shoulder across the front of the school. Inside, teachers tried to maintain calm and order. They read a bulletin to their homeroom classes. "We are to go about the business of teaching and learning," they said.

Elizabeth stepped off the bus across the street from the school and looked into a sea of hostile white faces. Some of the protesters waved Confederate flags, defiant symbols of the segregated South. Others held signs that read "KKK" or "Go back to Africa."

Crossing the street with quick, determined steps, Elizabeth walked toward the school entrance. When she reached the line of soldiers, they raised their rifles inches from her face. Trembling, but with her head held high, Elizabeth tried to find an opening in the line. But the soldiers would not let her pass. "Go to your own school, nigger!" someone in the crowd yelled.

Fighting back tears, Elizabeth turned, crossed the street and walked back to the bus stop. The mob followed, taunting her. "Get a rope! Let's lynch her!" they shouted.

Frozen with fear, Elizabeth sat on a bench, notebook on her lap, eyes straight ahead. Benjamin Fine, a white reporter for *The New York Times*, sat next to the terrified teenager and put his arm protectively around her. "Don't let them see you cry," he said.

Then a white-haired woman pushed her way through the crowd. "Stop! She's just a child!" she cried. The woman was

Grace Lorch, a white NAACP member. She led Elizabeth to a nearby drugstore so they could call a taxi.

The two were pushed and shoved, then prevented from entering the store. Then the mob turned on Fine, calling out insults and spitting on him. Finally a bus came, and Grace and Elizabeth boarded. For weeks Elizabeth would awaken, screaming, from nightmares about the incident.

As the other black students approached Central, Daisy heard a report on her car radio that a black girl was being mobbed at the school. Her heart sank when she realized it was Elizabeth. Daisy had forgotten to contact the Eckfords.

When the group arrived at Central, the soldiers barred their way as well. People in the crowd jeered at the black teenagers. "We don't want you here!" they shouted. The black students got back into the police cars and went home.

Quickly the NAACP turned to the district court judge, who asked President Dwight D. Eisenhower to order an investigation of the governor's actions. Faubus was enraged. "As commander-in-chief of the state militia, I have the authority to maintain order here," he told the president in a telegram.

On Thursday the Little Rock Nine stayed away from Central, where soldiers remained on patrol. Eisenhower sent a telegram to Faubus. "I took an oath to support and defend the Constitution," the president said, and he asked the governor to cooperate. But Faubus refused to remove his troops. Arkansas was now in defiance of a federal order.

STANDOFF AT CENTRAL HIGH

For the next several days it was quiet at Central High. Classes continued as soldiers patrolled the school grounds. The Little Rock Nine met at Daisy's, where they worked on assignments she was able to get from their teachers.

Letters and telegrams began to flood in from all over the world. The teenagers were amazed to learn that the crisis had made headlines in places as far away as Moscow and Rome.

Behind the scenes there was a flurry of legal and political activity as the NAACP and local officials tried to end the standoff between the Arkansas governor and the federal government. Faubus won instant support from segregationists, who proclaimed him a hero. Others condemned his use of military force to prevent integration. "We did not need the Guard," declared an angry Mayor Mann. "Faubus has caused trouble where there wasn't any."

A week after the Guard was called out to Central High, the Justice Department said it would seek a court order to make the governor remove the troops and allow desegregation to proceed. In the meantime, Brooks Hays, a U.S. congressman from Little Rock, proposed that Faubus and Eisenhower discuss the problem. On Saturday, September 14, a military helicopter carrying the Arkansas governor landed on the lawn of Eisenhower's vacation home in Newport, Rhode Island.

The two men talked briefly, then held a two-hour session in the president's office with several government officials, including U.S. Attorney General Herbert Brownell. Faubus asked that Little Rock be allowed to postpone integration. Eisenhower refused. Faubus seemed to accept the president's words. On Monday morning, however, the Guard was still at Central.

The week passed. At the court hearing on the injunction against him, Faubus defended his actions. He said that hundreds of protesters "armed to the teeth with repeating rifles" would have shown up at the high school if he had not called out the Guard.

But a Federal Bureau of Investigation (FBI) review of his actions had concluded that such claims were rumors. The governor was ordered to remove his troops at once.

On Sunday night, September 22, police and school officials met with Daisy to discuss protection for the nine teenagers when they attended school the next day. They decided that a detachment of state and local police would be dispatched to Central High and a police escort would be provided for the students.

Monday morning dawned bright and crisp, a beautiful early autumn day. The nine students met at Daisy's and said a prayer together. They were quiet and apprehensive. Would their school year finally begin?

At the high school a crowd was forming, and by 8:30 A.M. there were more than a thousand protesters. Assistant police chief Eugene Smith, a Central High graduate, spotted several known troublemakers. Most of the faces, however, were those of strangers. Had the governor encouraged these out-of-towners to show up, he wondered.

A cry was heard: "Here they come!" But it was not the nine students. Four black reporters had been mistaken for parents of the Little Rock Nine. The mob went after the journalists, hitting them with bricks. One reporter, James Hicks, was bent over double in pain while an enraged white man continued to kick him in the stomach.

The mob outside Central High on September 23 brutally assaulted several journalists, mistaking them for parents of the black students.

While the crowd was focused on the black reporters, the black students hurried into the side door of the school. When the mob realized what had happened, hysteria broke out. "Oh my God, they're in!" a woman screamed, bursting into tears.

The crowd broke through the police barricades. Raising their billy clubs, the officers tried unsuccessfully to hold the protesters. Next the mob turned on the group of white journalists from *Life* magazine, pushing them down and smashing their equipment.

The black students stood nervously in the hall. Thelma, who had a heart condition, suddenly felt her legs give way. The others scrambled to hold her up. "I've come this far," said Thelma, when it was suggested she return home. "I'm not giving up now."

During the morning a few white students walked out of their classes as the black students entered. Cruel comments were made. Other white students offered encouragement and later told reporters they were disgusted with the adults who were causing the trouble. But the police could no longer hold back the mob. At noon the Little Rock Nine were removed from Central High for their own protection. They were rushed out a delivery entrance and into waiting police cars.

That night there was violence across the city. Windows were shattered by bricks and bottles, and blacks were pulled from their vehicles and beaten. The police made many arrests. Daisy's house was placed under armed guard, and L. C. carried a loaded pistol. A car that was observed driving past the Bateses' home was stopped. In it police found a bundle of dynamite.

The violence greatly saddened Mayor Mann. "We are a disgraced city because of a handful of people," he said. Daisy, too, was upset. She decided that the Little Rock Nine would not return to Central until their protection was guaranteed by the president of the United States.

7

THE SCREAMING EAGLES

President Eisenhower was worried. The situation in Little Rock was growing worse, but he was reluctant to use the force of the federal government to resolve the crisis. The president was not a strong supporter of desegregation. It was said that he disagreed with the *Brown* decision and may have even tried to pressure Chief Justice Warren to vote against the case.

Still, the president realized his responsibility was to see that the law of the land was upheld, regardless of his personal feelings. When Little Rock's officials began asking him to intercede in the crisis, Eisenhower issued an emergency proclamation on September 23.

On national television he called the situation in Arkansas a disgrace. If resistance to desegregation does not end, the president warned, "I will use my full power to see that the federal order is carried out."

The next morning nearly two thousand protesters stood outside Central High School, heckling and booing the police. "You can't make us integrate!" they shouted. The Little Rock Nine stayed home. Both Congressman Hays and Mayor Mann sent telegrams to Washington. "The situation is out of control," the messages read. "Send help."

The president had no choice but to act. In his Newport office he picked up a pen and, as his aides looked on, he signed a historic document. It authorized Secretary of Defense Charles Wilson to send armed troops to Little Rock.

Eisenhower then placed the entire Arkansas National Guard, some ten thousand soldiers, under federal order, removing them from the governor's control. This time the soldiers would be used to enforce integration, not to prevent the black children from entering their school, as they had done three weeks earlier.

Within minutes Wilson ordered one thousand paratroopers from Fort Campbell, Kentucky, to Little Rock. They would travel in eight huge military transport planes to the Air Force base there.

The troopers were part of the elite 101st Airborne Division of the 327th Infantry Regiment. Known as the Screaming Eagles, the unit included men who had fought at the Battle of the Bulge in World War II. Major General Edwin A. Walker was placed in command of all the troops in the Arkansas mission.

By early evening the deep drone of the transport planes could be heard over Little Rock. Soon the first of a long line of military vehicles began to enter the city. Sirens wailed and lights flashed as local police cars escorted the convoy to Central High.

The 101st Airborne included many black soldiers, but they were kept on reserve at the Little Rock Armory. Their presence at Central High might only further agitate an unruly mob.

Rifles, ammunition, bayonets, clubs, tear gas canisters, gas masks, food, bedding, and communications equipment were unloaded at the school. The troopers went quickly to their tasks.

Troops from the 101st Airborne Division roll into
Little Rock on the night of September 24.

They unreeled wire and strung communications lines from trees that normally shaded teachers and students. Pup tents and field kitchens were set up near the tennis courts. Troopers stood in small groups on the landscaped lawn, poring over maps of Central and the surrounding areas. Soon every entrance was secured.

On television the president was addressing the nation from the Oval Office. He explained his reasons for sending federal troops to Little Rock. "Mob rule cannot be allowed to override the decisions of our courts," he declared.

With these words Eisenhower became the first president since the post-Civil War period known as Reconstruction to use federal force to support black rights. He would not be the last.

After the president's address, Daisy was told the Little Rock Nine were to attend school the next day. All the families had to be notified, but because of constant harassment they had begun taking their phones off the hook at bedtime.

Daisy set out at midnight to visit the nine houses that were scattered all over Little Rock. It took her three hours to see all the families. She found them fearful, angry, and worried that their children would be subjected to yet more violence.

But by 8:25 A.M. on Wednesday, all nine teenagers waited at Daisy's for their military escort. Finally there was a knock on the door. Daisy opened it to an army officer, who saluted her. "Mrs. Bates," he said, "we're ready for the children."

As soldiers stand guard outside the Bates home, the girls enter a station wagon for the ride to school on September 25.

At Central, a third of the two thousand white students were missing, kept home by their parents in protest or because they feared violence. Once the Little Rock Nine were inside the school, most of the other white students seemed to accept their presence. Some even invited the black teenagers to have lunch with them.

But the trouble was far from over. The phone rang that morning in the principal's office. "Your school will be blown up at noon," the caller warned. Central High was evacuated and a demolition squad was summoned to search the building, but no bomb was found. The students returned to their classes.

When the last bell rang at 3:00 P.M., the nine, flanked by paratroopers, left quietly through a side door. Hundreds more soldiers surrounded the school, keeping onlookers at a distance.

Reporters flocked around the departing white students. "How did the day go?" they asked. "It went fine," said one student. "If only the parents would go home and leave us alone, we'd be all right."

The black students were driven back to Daisy's, where they reflected on their first day at school. Though a small number of students had been openly hostile, others had been friendly and helpful, they said.

Daisy, however, was uneasy. She knew that many of the children of active segregationists had stayed home. What would happen when they returned to school? Would even the U.S. military be enough to protect the Little Rock Nine?

CAMPAIGN OF HATE

Faubus may have lost one battle, but he did not intend to lose the war. He had returned from a governors' conference incensed that Eisenhower had intervened on behalf of the nine black students.

During the next few days it appeared that integration might proceed without further incident. Hundreds of Central students remained at home. Under the watchful eyes of the troopers, the school held its first integrated assembly on Friday. The gathering closed with the school song, which honored Central High's school colors. Its lyrics were ironic: "Hail to the Old Gold, Hail to the Black."

Soon trouble would be stirred up once more. Faubus had written a speech that would anger Little Rock residents and increase the tension and fear that enveloped the city. "We are now an occupied territory," he declared on television Friday evening.

The governor charged that the troopers were "bludgeoning innocent bystanders," and "spilling the warm red blood of a patriotic

American city." He failed to mention that the "innocent bystanders" had threatened the black students, injured both black and white reporters, and taunted the soldiers or refused to obey their orders.

If the segregationists could not prevent the Little Rock Nine from entering Central High, they could try to drive them out of the school. They would use their own children to make the atmosphere inside the school unwelcoming, and in many cases terrifying, for the black students.

In October a campaign of intimidation and hate began. Only about seventy-five white students were involved, but their efforts were relentless. They threw rocks at the black teenagers, called them names, tripped them, tossed eggs at them, knocked books from their hands, spit on them, vandalized their lockers, and tossed their belongings out of windows or into toilets.

Jefferson Thomas was attacked from behind by two white students and knocked unconscious. Ink was squirted on Gloria Ray's new dress. Carlotta Walls learned how to carry her books in such a way as to block a jab or punch. All of the nine began taking an extra set of clothing to school.

Prompted by the Mothers League, a group of white students staged a walkout and held a demonstration near the school. They lynched and burned a straw-stuffed effigy of a black student.

Melba Patillo was always terrified. "What have I done to deserve this?" she would think every time she was shoved or ridiculed. The only way she could climb the three long flights of stairs to her homeroom each day was by mouthing the words to the Lord's Prayer, over and over again.

Bomb threats were called into the school almost daily, and not all of them were pranks. A bottle bomb was found in one locker,

*Faubus displays the front
page of the conservative*
Manchester Union Leader
*during a television address
condemning what he called
the "occupation" of Little
Rock by federal troops.*

*White students
hung a black effigy
during a walkout
on October 3. Para-
troopers were called
in to break up the
demonstration.*

two sticks of dynamite in another. Rest room walls were covered with racial slurs. Eventually, any white students who had been friendly with the black teenagers were warned to stop or risk being beaten. The nine students felt more alone than ever.

All over Little Rock the segregationists made their message known. Crosses were burned on the lawns of black families and of white people who were calling for racial tolerance. Shots were fired at Daisy Bates's house and at Superintendent Blossom's car.

Though racial incidents continued inside the school, mob violence outside Central had been curbed. The number of paratroopers at Central was slowly reduced. The black students were no longer escorted to their classes by armed guards. They began riding to school in car pools rather than in military vehicles.

By the end of November the president had withdrawn the last of the 101st Airborne. Some three hundred National Guardsmen took their place. They would remain at Central for the rest of the year.

After the paratroopers left, hostility inside the high school increased. While the troopers had kept a close eye on the Little Rock Nine, the Guard seemed often to look the other way when the black students were in trouble.

The nine teenagers grew more fearful every day. But, inspired by the example of Martin Luther King, Jr., who believed in bringing about change through nonviolence, they tried hard to resist retaliating against their tormentors.

Much of the abuse was tolerated, if not ignored, by teachers and school administrators. School officials said they were overwhelmed by the number of discipline problems. A few were fair with the black students, but most openly opposed desegregation and would not go out of their way to make it work.

Ernest Green's physics teacher tried continually to discourage him. He refused to allow the senior to make up missing work from the first three weeks of school, would not give him extra help, and told him that the course was far too challenging "for a Negro." Fearful that he would fail, Ernest had to hire a tutor.

His troubles were not limited to the classroom. As Ernest stepped into the gym showers one day, he cut his foot on broken glass scattered on the floor by two white students. When he reported the incident, his gym teacher denied the glass was there and called Ernest a troublemaker.

Police and FBI agents were nearly always at Central, investigating each racial incident. The NAACP complained constantly to school officials that the abuse was being allowed to continue. Dozens of white students were suspended that year, but the attacks did not stop.

Minniejean Brown seemed to be singled out for torment. After months of being pushed, kicked, spit on, and insulted, she could no longer abide the humiliation. In December two white students tried to block her way in the cafeteria line. Minniejean dumped a bowl of chili on one of the boys. The black kitchen employees, silent for months, applauded. Minniejean was briefly suspended.

Other incidents involving Minniejean followed. In February, after she insulted a white girl who had been harassing her, Minniejean was expelled. She was offered a scholarship to the private New Lincoln School in New York City, where she lived with a college professor and his wife. The day after Minniejean's expulsion, small white cards were circulated inside Central. "One down, eight to go," they read.

In the spring there was relative calm at the school. The segregationists seemed to tire of their campaign, and racial attacks slowed. Then, as the end of the school year grew closer, a new wave of protest began.

Segregationists were determined to prevent the graduation of the first black student from Central High. They warned school officials that there might be trouble if Ernest attended commencement ceremonies.

Efforts were made to prevent any violence. Only people holding tickets would be admitted to the commencement exercises. Extra police would be on duty. More than one hundred soldiers would be stationed inside the stadium. FBI agents would be nearby.

Earnest began to receive threatening notes and phone calls. No black would ever graduate from Central, he was told, "even if we have to kill you." Attempts were made to provoke him to fight so that he might be expelled. What Ernest feared most, however, was not being allowed to march with his class.

But on May 27, he was one of 602 seniors assembled for Central High's commencement. He tried not to notice that the white students on both sides of him had moved their chairs several inches away.

Principal Matthews had taken Ernest aside prior to the ceremony. "You can go home if you want," he said. "It will be safer if we mail your diploma."

"I'm sorry," Ernest said. "My family came to see me graduate and I won't disappoint them."

From the podium Matthews addressed the audience. He praised the school's honor students and congratulated its athletic teams for their accomplishments. But he never mentioned the courage and determination of Ernest Green and of the other eight black teenagers who had made history at Central High that year.

Ernest Green became the first black student to graduate from Central High.

ERNEST GREEN

IN 1958, Ernest Green became the first black student to graduate from Central High School in Little Rock, Arkansas. He had wanted to attend the all-white school because he knew he would get a better education there.

He endured cruel and degrading treatment during his year at Central High. "I'll never forget it," he said in an interview. "It was a war of nerves, like being in combat." But Green never gave up. "I was determined to make it through," he declared.

Green came from a family in which he was "taught to meet all challenges," he said. His mother, Lothaire, a teacher, and his grandfather, Eugene Scott, a mail carrier, valued education.

After graduating from Central High, Green attended Michigan State University on a full scholarship and earned bachelor's and master's degrees in sociology. He worked in New York City with an organization that sought to get more black people into apprenticeships in the building trades.

Green served as President Jimmy Carter's assistant secretary of labor for employment and training from 1976 to 1980. He then became a managing director in the public finance division of Lehman Brothers, an investment banking firm in Washington, D.C., and served on the national board of the NAACP.

He has returned to Central High School many times. In 1987, Green delivered the school's baccalaureate address during its commencement exercises. A made-for-television movie about his historic role in the desegregation of Central High was premiered at the school in early 1993. Among the guests at the premier was President Bill Clinton, a former governor of Arkansas.

When diplomas were awarded, there were cheers and applause as each student rose and walked to the front. Then Ernest heard his name called. Except for a spattering of applause, the crowd was silent. He made his way alone, down the aisle, up the stairs, and across the platform. All the while he thought, "I am walking not only for me but for all nine of us."

Ernest had accomplished what he had set out to do. He had graduated from Central High School. When the jubilant teenager joined his mother, grandfather, other family members, and Daisy Bates after the ceremony, he was congratulated by another, very special guest who had accompanied the group—the Reverend Martin Luther King, Jr.

AFTER THE CRISIS

The first phase of school integration in Little Rock was over, but it would take many more years to bring about complete desegregation. Early in 1958, the school board had asked the U.S. district court to delay further integration in Little Rock until 1961.

The district court judge noted the violence that had occurred at Central and the need for military assistance. He pointed out that the educational process had been disrupted. Then he agreed that integration should be postponed.

NAACP attorneys succeeded in getting the decision overturned. But the school board took the case to the Supreme Court, where deliberations went on for months. Thurgood Marshall fought hard for integration to continue without interruption. A delay would only send a message to segregationists that violence works, he said.

That summer Faubus was nominated for a third term as governor. Soon after, he recommended several bills to the Arkansas legislature. One gave the governor the authority to close public schools if violence was expected. All of the bills passed.

On September 12, the Supreme Court ruled that integration must proceed immediately. Little Rock schools were to open three days later. Two hours after the ruling, Faubus, defiant once more, signed an order that closed the city's public high schools to avoid desegregation. Nearly four thousand students were affected.

Under the governor's direction, a private segregated school was opened in October. Donated funds were used to lease a building for the project. The school eventually enrolled eight hundred white students. Most of the other high school students attended private schools or transferred to public schools in districts outside the city. Several hundred teenagers did not attend school that year, though some took correspondence courses.

The city was torn apart, its reputation damaged, and its public school system nearly destroyed. The following summer, the Supreme Court ruled that the closing of Little Rock's public schools was unconstitutional and that integration must proceed. A few days later a bomb was hurled at the Bateses' house, falling short and forming a crater in the front yard.

The reopening of schools was set for August 12, 1959. There would be no paratroopers or National Guard, only local police and fire fighters. On the evening before school was to begin, Faubus appeared on television. He warned that violence would not accomplish anything, but he reminded residents that integration was being forced on Little Rock.

The next morning hundreds of protesters from across Arkansas gathered on the steps of the State Capitol. They stood in the hot sun waving flags and shouting "We want Faubus!" The governor finally appeared and spoke briefly, again cautioning that violence was not a good idea. But other speakers urged the crowd to resist integration. Then some two hundred people turned and began marching the fifteen blocks to Central High.

Opponents of school desegregation demonstrate outside the Arkansas State Capitol.

Five men in front carried American flags. Others held Confederate flags and signs that read "Keep Central White!" A sound truck played "Dixie." As the crowd got closer to the school, the protesters began their favorite chant: "Two, four, six, eight! We don't want to integrate!"

They reached the line of police and fire fighters two blocks from the school. Chief Smith held a portable electric megaphone. "Your behavior is a disgrace!" he told them. "Get out of the street!" Instead, the mob tried to push through the barricade. Several people were grabbed and hustled into patrol cars. Billy clubs were used on others. Powerful fire hoses were turned on the rest.

The police remained at the school for the rest of the week, but there were no further incidents. The crisis at Central High was over. The dramatic conflict, however, would leave its mark on many who were involved in it.

Mayor Mann left Little Rock, as did Superintendent Blossom, whose contract was bought out by the school board. In 1960 Chief Smith shot and killed his wife and himself. Some believed the stress of the desegregation crisis may have contributed to the tragedy.

Elizabeth Eckford's mother lost her job as a teacher. Carlotta Walls's father, a brick mason, could no longer find work in the Little Rock area when word spread that his daughter was among the students who integrated Central High.

Daisy and L. C. Bates, who in the 1940s had founded *The Arkansas State Press*, a weekly newspaper for black residents, lost several advertising accounts from local businesses during the crisis, and the paper folded in 1959. (It resumed publication in the 1980s.) Daisy remained active in the NAACP. In 1958, she and the Little Rock Nine were awarded the NAACP's prestigious Spingarn Medal for their pioneering role in school desegregation.

Harassment continued when schools reopened in 1959. Here Jefferson Thomas, waiting for a bus, is jeered by a crowd outside the corner drugstore.

A Gallup poll in late 1958 placed Governor Faubus among the ten most admired men in America. He would be reelected in 1960, 1962, and 1964. Later in life Faubus modified his views on racial issues.

Only Ernest, Carlotta, and Jefferson graduated from Central High. Elizabeth and Thelma, who as seniors had taken correspondence courses during the year the high schools were closed, received certificates of graduation. Melba, Terrance, and Gloria transferred to high schools in other states. Minniejean received her diploma from New Lincoln School in New York City.

All nine attended college, and some earned master's degrees. Melba went on to head a public relations firm in San Francisco. Minniejean began a career as a writer. Terrance became an assistant dean in the School of Social Welfare at the University of California at Los Angeles. Carlotta joined a real estate firm in Denver, and Gloria the staff of a magazine in Europe.

Thelma became a public school counselor in Illinois, and Jefferson an accountant with the U.S. government. Elizabeth, the only one of the original nine students to remain in Little Rock, is a U.S. Army veteran. After serving as President Jimmy Carter's assistant secretary of labor, Ernest joined an investment banking firm in Washington, D.C.

In the fall of 1987 the Little Rock Nine held an emotional reunion at Central High. Accompanied by their families, the nine were given a hero's welcome, a far cry from their experience thirty years earlier.

After the crisis in Little Rock, desegregation proceeded slowly in the South. Ten years later, 68 percent of southern black children were still in segregated schools. Central High was not the last place the U.S. military was sent to enforce desegregation. President John F. Kennedy dispatched troops to the University of Mississippi in 1962 and to the University of Alabama a year later, when Governor George Wallace personally barred two black students from entering.

Eventually all public schools in Little Rock were integrated. In 1993 the school district's enrollment was 64 percent African American. Diversity now characterizes Central and the city's four other public high schools. More than half of Central's two thousand students are black, as are one third of its teachers. The school has had four black principals.

Although many years have passed since *Brown* v. *Board of Education of Topeka*, desegregation is still an issue in school districts in both the South and the North. Inner-city schools that serve mostly minority students are often underfunded and overcrowded, and they lack the resources of suburban schools. Several lawsuits have been brought against state governments by civil rights groups in an effort to correct the problem.

The battle for full racial equality is not over. But laws are not enough to solve the problem of discrimination, many people believe. "The courts can't change how white people think about blacks," Daisy Bates has said. "They have to change themselves."

Chronology

1954   *Brown* v. *Board of Education of Topeka* ends segregation in America's public schools

1955   U.S. Supreme Court orders integration to proceed "with all deliberate speed"

1956   NAACP asks U.S. district court to force immediate and complete desegregation in Little Rock

1957   Little Rock School Board ordered to begin integration of Central High

September 3: Governor Faubus calls out National Guard to prevent desegregation of Central High School

September 4: Mob chases Elizabeth Eckford away from Central High; other black students barred from entering

September 20: Governor Faubus ordered to remove Guard

September 23: Little Rock Nine enter Central under police protection but are removed at noon

September 24: President Eisenhower sends the 101st Airborne to Little Rock

September 25: Little Rock Nine spend first full day at Central High

101st Airborne withdrawn by end of November; replaced by National Guard

1958   February: Minniejean Brown expelled

May: Ernest Brown graduates from Central High

1958–1959   Little Rock public high schools are closed for the entire school year

1959   August: High schools reopen and integration proceeds

Sources

Sources for *Little Rock: The Desegregation of Central High* included reference books, histories, autobiographies and biographies, periodicals, oral histories, and interviews. All the quotations used in this book derive from them.

Particularly helpful to the author were conversations with two of the Little Rock Nine, Carlotta Walls LaNier and Ernest Green, and Jeannette Wagner of the Little Rock School District.

A complete list of sources follows:

Adler, Mortimer J., ed. *The Negro in American History*. New York: Encyclopaedia Britannica Educational Corp., 1969.

Bardolph, Richard. *The Civil Rights Record*. New York: Thomas Y. Crowell Company, 1970.

Bates, Daisy. *The Long Shadow of Little Rock: A Memoir*. New York: David McKay Co., Inc., 1962.

Blossom, Virgil T. *It Has Happened Here*. New York: Harper & Brothers, 1959.

Davis, Michael D., and Hunter R. Clark. *Thurgood Marshall: Warrior at the Bar, Rebel on the Bench*. New York: Carol Publishing Group, 1992.

Faber, Doris, and Harold Faber. *We the People*. New York: Charles Scribner's Sons, 1987.

Freyer, Tony. *The Little Rock Crisis: A Constitutional Interpretation*. Westport, Ct.: Greenwood Press, 1984.

Goldston, Robert. *The Negro Revolution*. New York: The Macmillan Company, 1968.

Hampton, Henry, and Steve Fayer. *Voices of Freedom: An Oral History of the Civil Rights Movement from the 1950s through the 1980s*. New York: Bantam Books, 1990.

Huckaby, Elizabeth. *Crisis at Central High*. Baton Rouge: Louisiana State University Press, 1980.

Humphrey, Hubert H., ed. *School Desegregation. Documents and Commentaries*. New York: Thomas Y. Crowell Co., 1964.

Irons, Peter. *The Courage of their Convictions*. New York: The Free Press, 1988.

Katz, William Loren. *Eyewitness. The Negro in American History*. New York: Pitman Publishing Corp., 1967.

"The Meaning of Little Rock." *Time*. Oct. 7, 1957, pp. 21–25.

Newton, Michael, and Judy Ann Newton. *Racial and Religious Violence in America*. New York: Garland Publishing Inc., 1991.

Powledge, Fred. *Free At Last? The Civil Rights Movement and the People Who Made It*. Boston: Little, Brown and Co., 1991.

Record, Wilson, and Jane C. Record. *Little Rock, U.S.A. Materials for Analysis*. San Francisco: Chandler Publishing Co., 1960.

Rowan, Carl T. *Dream Makers, Dream Breakers*. Boston: Little, Brown and Co., 1993.

Sarratt, Reed. *The Ordeal of Desegregation: The First Decade*. New York: Harper & Row, 1966.

Silverman, Corinne. *The Little Rock Story. Inter-University Case Program Number 41*. New York: The Bobbs-Merrill Co., Inc., 1959.

Sitkoff, Harvard. *The Struggle for Black Equality*. New York: Hill and Wang, 1981.

Sterling, Dorothy. *Tear Down the Walls: A History of the American Civil Rights Movement*. New York: Doubleday & Co., Inc., 1968.

Wakefield, Dan. *Revolt in the South*. New York: Grove Press, 1960.

"What Orval Hath Wrought." *Time*. Sept. 23, 1957, pp. 11–17.

Wilkinson, J. Harvie III. *From Brown to Bakke: The Supreme Court and School Integration: 1954–1978*. New York: Oxford University Press, 1979.

Williams, Juan. *Eyes on the Prize*. New York: Viking Penguin Inc., 1987.

Further Reading

Edwards, Audrey, and Craig K. Polite. *Children of the Dream*.
New York: Doubleday & Co., 1992.

Hamilton, Virginia. *Many Thousand Gone: African Americans from
Slavery to Freedom*. New York: Alfred A. Knopf, 1993.

Kosof, Anna. *The Civil Rights Movement and Its Legacy*. New
York: Franklin Watts, 1989.

Levine, Ellen. *Freedom's Children*. New York: G. P. Putnam's
Sons, 1993.

Myers, Walter Dean. *Now Is Your Time*. New York: Harper-
Collins, 1991.

Turner, Glennette. *Take a Walk in Their Shoes*. New York: Puf-
fin Books, 1992.

Woodward, C. Vann. *The Strange Career of Jim Crow*. New York:
Oxford University Press, 1974.

Index